Social Security Made Simple

Social Security Retirement Benefits and
Related Planning Topics
Explained in 100 Pages or Less

Social Security Made Simple

Social Security Retirement Benefits and
Related Planning Topics
Explained in 100 Pages or Less

Mike Piper, CPA

Dedication

For you, the reader, so that you can get the benefits you deserve from the system that you've paid into for so many years.

Why is there a light bulb on the cover?

In cartoons and comics, a light bulb is often used to signify a moment of clarity or sudden understanding—an "aha!" moment. My hope is that the books in the *...in 100 Pages or Less* series can help readers achieve clarity and understanding of topics that are often considered complex and confusing—hence the light bulb.

Disclaimer

This book is not intended to be a substitute for personalized advice from a professional financial planner. Nothing contained within this text should be construed as financial advice. The publisher and author make no representation or warranty as to this book's adequacy or appropriateness for any purpose. Similarly, no representation or warranty is made as to the accuracy of the material in this book.

Purchasing this book does not create any client relationship or other advisory, fiduciary, or professional services relationship with the publisher or with the author. *You alone* bear the *sole* responsibility of assessing the merits and risks associated with any financial decisions you make. And it should always be kept in mind that any investment can result in partial or complete loss.

Your Feedback Is Appreciated!

As the author of this book, I'm very interested to hear your thoughts. If you find the book helpful, please let me know! Alternatively, if you have any suggestions of ways to make the book better, I'm eager to hear that, too.

Finally, if you're dissatisfied with your purchase for any reason, let me know, and I'll be happy to provide you with a refund of the current list price of the book (limited to one refund per household).

You can reach me at: mike@simplesubjects.com.

Best Regards,
Mike Piper, CPA

Table of Contents

Part Two
Rules for Less Common Situations

Part Three
Social Security Planning:
When to Claim Benefits

Part Four
Other Related Planning Topics

INTRODUCTION

The Benefits of Understanding Your Benefits

According to the Social Security Administration, Social Security benefits make up more than 30% of the income of U.S. citizens age 65 or older. Unfortunately, it's common for retirees to make decisions regarding their Social Security benefits that cause them to miss out on tens of thousands of dollars (or sometimes even a six-figure sum) over the course of their retirement.

Assuming that you anticipate Social Security benefits playing a meaningful role in your retirement finances, it's important for you to understand how the system works and what you can do to get the most out of your benefits.

What We'll Be Covering

This book is organized into four sections. Part 1 covers the basic rules: how retirement benefits are calculated, how spousal benefits are calculated, and how widow(er) benefits are calculated. Part 2 takes a look at the rules for a handful of slightly less common situations—when you or your spouse have a pension from government work, for instance. Part

3 discusses the question of when to start taking Social Security benefits and provides a few strategies for getting the most out of your benefits. Part 4 covers some related planning topics such as tax planning opportunities that arise as a result of the unique way in which Social Security benefits are taxed.

But Won't the Rules Change?

When Social Security was first created, it covered a much smaller group of workers; it did not provide for spousal benefits or widow(er) benefits; it did not allow for retirement benefits prior to age 65; and benefits weren't subject to federal income tax at all. In other words, Social Security originally looked quite different than it looks today.

More recently, the Bipartisan Budget Act of 2015 made significant changes to the Social Security strategies that will be available to people going forward.

It's a sure bet that the Social Security system will continue to evolve in the future. But there's no way to know when the rules will change, for whom they will change, or what those changes will be. So, for lack of any other reasonable option, this book is written based on the rules as they stand now.

If, however, you're working on your retirement plan and you want to make an adjustment to your projected Social Security benefits to account for the program's financial troubles, the 2018 Social

Security Trustees Report may be of use.[1] The report projected that there will be sufficient funds to cover 100% of benefits promised under the current system until 2034, after which point there will only be enough money to pay for approximately 77% of projected benefits. Does that mean that benefits will go unchanged for the next fifteen years, then drop across the board, all at once, by 23%? Probably not. What actually *will* happen? Your guess is as good as mine.

Let's Keep This Brief

As with the other books in the *...in 100 Pages or Less* series, the goal of this book is a modest one: to provide an introduction to the aspects of Social Security that are most likely to factor into your retirement planning. In other words, this book is *not* intended to turn you into a Social Security expert. Nor is it intended to serve as a 100%-comprehensive guide to every aspect of Social Security.[2]

---

[1] The report is available at:
ssa.gov/oact/tr/2018/tr2018.pdf

[2] For example, disability-related benefits are not covered in this book. If you're interested in a book that *does* cover those benefits, I'd recommend *Social Security: The Inside Story* by Andy Landis.

PART ONE

Social Security Basics

Qualifying for Retirement Benefits

To be eligible for Social Security retirement benefits, you must:

1. Be age 62 or older, and
2. Have earned 40 Social Security "credits" over the course of your career. [1]

Attaining Age 62

The first month for which you can receive a benefit payment is the first month in which you are age 62 for the entire month. This means that, for most people, the first month for which you can receive a

---

[1] If you become disabled prior to age 62, it's possible to qualify for retirement benefits with fewer than 40 credits.

retirement benefit is the month *after* the month including your 62nd birthday. If, however, your 62nd birthday is on the first or second day of the month, you are considered to be age 62 for that entire month.

Earning Social Security Credits

Social Security credits are earned by working at a job where you pay Social Security taxes or by earning money from self-employment. The amount of earnings needed to earn a credit is adjusted each year in keeping with wage inflation. For 2019, you receive one credit for each $1,360 of covered income that you earn during the year.

Credits are sometimes called "quarters of coverage" because you can earn a maximum of four per year. To earn four credits in a given year, however, you do not actually have to work in each of the four calendar quarters. For instance, if you earned $5,440 in January of 2019 and did not work for the rest of the year, you would still earn four credits for the year.

"Eligible" vs. "Entitled"

In Social Security jargon, the words "eligible" and "entitled" mean different things. You are *eligible* for a given type of benefit once you meet all of the requirements to be able to file for it. Then, once you do actually file for that benefit, you become *entitled* to it. (As we'll discuss in Chapter 3, however, filing can happen automatically in some cases.)

Chapter 1 Simple Summary

- Unless you become disabled prior to age 62, in order to qualify for Social Security retirement benefits you must be 62 years old, and you must have earned at least 40 "credits."

- You can earn a maximum of four Social Security credits per year.

- In 2019, you earn one Social Security credit for each $1,360 of income you earn that is subject to Social Security taxes.

- You are *eligible* for a given type of benefit once you meet the requirements to be able to file for it. You become *entitled* to a benefit once you do actually file for it.

CHAPTER TWO

How Retirement Benefits Are Calculated

The size of your monthly retirement benefit depends on:

1. Your earnings history, and
2. How old you are when you first begin taking benefits.[1]

But first we need to back up a step. In order to understand how Social Security benefits are calculated, you need to be familiar with two terms:

- "full retirement age" (FRA), and
- "primary insurance amount" (PIA).

---

[1] It can depend on other factors as well, such as your current earnings if you have a job while you're collecting Social Security. But for simplicity's sake, let's start with the most basic scenario.

4

Your full retirement age depends on the year in which you were born (see table below). Your primary insurance amount is the amount of retirement benefits you would receive per month if you started taking them at your full retirement age. As we'll discuss shortly, your PIA is determined by your earnings history.

Year of Birth[1]	Full Retirement Age
1937 or earlier	65
1938	65 and 2 months
1939	65 and 4 months
1940	65 and 6 months
1941	65 and 8 months
1942	65 and 10 months
1943-1954	66
1955	66 and 2 months
1956	66 and 4 months
1957	66 and 6 months
1958	66 and 8 months
1959	66 and 10 months
1960 or later	67

---

[1] If your birthday is January 1st, you will be treated as if you were born in the prior year for the purpose of determining your full retirement age.

How Earnings History Affects Retirement Benefits

Your primary insurance amount is based on your historical earnings. Specifically, it's based on your "average indexed monthly earnings" (AIME). Calculating your AIME is a five-step process.

1. Make a year-by-year list of your earnings, excluding any earnings for each year that were in excess of the maximum amount subject to Social Security tax.[1]
2. Adjust your earnings from prior years to today's dollars.[2]
3. Select your 35 highest-earning years.
4. Add up the total amount of earnings in those 35 years.
5. Divide by 420 (the number of months in 35 years).

You do not actually have to do this calculation yourself. The Social Security Administration does it for

---

[1] For historical maximums by year, see: ssa.gov/planners/maxtax.htm

[2] Specifically, earnings from years prior to the year in which you reach age 60 are adjusted for the growth in the national average wage that occurred between the year in which you earned the money and the year in which you reached age 60. Earnings from years after you reach age 60 are included in the calculation at their actual dollar amount.

you. It is, however, important to understand the concept, so that you can understand how your benefit is calculated.

Calculating Your Primary Insurance Amount

For someone becoming eligible for retirement benefits (that is, reaching age 62) in 2019, his or her primary insurance amount would be:

- 90% of any AIME up to $926, plus
- 32% of any AIME between $926 and $5,583, plus
- 15% of any AIME above $5,583.[1]

Or, to put it in terms of annual income, if claimed at full retirement age, Social Security would replace:

- 90% of the first $11,112 of average annual wage-inflation-adjusted earnings, plus
- 32% of average annual wage-inflation-adjusted earnings from $11,112 to $66,996, plus

---

[1] These figures, referred to as "bend points," change to account for wage inflation each year. So, for example, for somebody turning age 62 in 2020, each of these dollar amounts will probably be slightly higher.

- 15% of average annual wage-inflation-adjusted earnings from $66,996 to $123,552.

Two noteworthy takeaways here are that:

1. Social Security replaces a higher portion of wages for lower-earning workers than for higher-earning workers, and
2. There's a maximum possible Social Security retirement benefit. (Few people reach that maximum though, because doing so would require that you earn the maximum earnings subject to Social Security tax for 35 different years.)

If You Worked Fewer than 35 Years

If you have fewer than 35 years in which you earned income subject to Social Security taxes, the calculation of your average indexed monthly earnings will include zeros. For example, if you worked for 31 years, your AIME calculation would include those 31 years of earnings, as well as 4 years of zeros.

As a result, working additional years would result in those zero-earnings years being knocked out of the calculation and replaced with your current earnings. The result isn't going to make you rich, but it's worth including in your list of considerations when deciding when to retire.

How Age Affects Retirement Benefits

If you wait until *after* full retirement age to claim your retirement benefit, the amount you receive will be greater than your primary insurance amount. The increase is $2/3$ of 1% of your PIA for each month you wait beyond full retirement age (up to age 70, beyond which there is no increase for waiting). This works out to an increase of 8% per year.

EXAMPLE: Alan was born in 1954, so his full retirement age is 66. His primary insurance amount is $2,000. If he waits until age 70 (that is, 48 months after FRA) to claim his retirement benefit, he will receive $2,640 per month, calculated as:

- His PIA of $2,000 per month, plus
- $2/3$ of 1% x 48 months x $2,000.

If you claim your retirement benefit *prior* to full retirement age, it will be reduced from your primary insurance amount by $5/9$ of 1% for each month (up to 36 months) prior to full retirement age. This works out to a reduction of 6.67% per year. For each month in excess of 36 months, the reduction is $5/12$ of 1% (or 5% per year).

EXAMPLE: Allison was born in 1960, so her full retirement age is 67. Her primary insurance amount is $2,000. If she claims retirement benefits at age

9

65 (24 months prior to FRA), her monthly benefit would be $1,733.33, calculated as:

- Her PIA of $2,000 per month, minus
- $5/9$ of 1% x 24 months x $2,000.[1]

If Allison decides instead to claim at age 62 (60 months prior to her FRA), her benefit would be $1,400 per month, calculated as:

- Her PIA of $2,000 per month, minus
- $5/9$ of 1% x 36 months x $2,000, minus
- $5/12$ of 1% x 24 months x $2,000.

In short, the interaction between the size of your retirement benefit and the age at which you first claim that benefit looks like this:

---

[1] Allison would actually receive $1,733 per month, because the Social Security Administration rounds all monthly benefit payments *down* to the next lower multiple of $1.

Age when you claim retirement benefits	Amount of retirement benefit[1]
5 years before FRA	70% of PIA
4 years before FRA	75% of PIA
3 years before FRA	80% of PIA
2 years before FRA	86.67% of PIA
1 year before FRA	93.33% of PIA
at FRA	100% of PIA
1 year after FRA	108% of PIA
2 years after FRA	116% of PIA
3 years after FRA	124% of PIA
4 years after FRA	132% of PIA

Adjusting Benefits for Inflation

Every year after you reach age 62, your primary insurance amount is adjusted to keep up with inflation as measured by the Consumer Price Index for Urban Wage Earners and Clerical Workers (CPI-W). When your PIA is adjusted upward for inflation, it increases not only your retirement benefit, but also any other benefits that are based on your

---

[1] Please note that the increases and decreases are actually based on *months* before or after full retirement age, rather than years. So the actual amount you receive will probably be between two of the figures listed in this table. In addition, as mentioned above, the actual formulas use fractions rather than decimals, which could result in slightly different amounts.

PIA (e.g., your spouse's spousal benefit or widow/widower benefit if your spouse should outlive you).[1]

For brevity's sake, I will be writing in "today's dollars" throughout this book. In other words, rather than explicitly mentioning in nearly every single paragraph that the benefit(s) discussed would be adjusted for inflation, I will simply write what the benefit would be, as measured today. Please understand that, from there, the benefit would be adjusted annually in keeping with inflation.

---

[1] Contrary to a common misconception, CPI-W *does* account for changes in the prices of food and energy.

Chapter 2 Simple Summary

- Your "primary insurance amount" (PIA) is the monthly retirement benefit you would receive if you claimed benefits at "full retirement age" (FRA).

- Your primary insurance amount is calculated based on your 35 highest-earning years (after adjusting prior years' earnings for wage inflation).

- If you claim retirement benefits prior to your full retirement age, you will receive an amount smaller than your PIA. If you wait until after your full retirement age to claim benefits, your retirement benefit will be greater than your PIA.

- Social Security benefits are adjusted on an annual basis to keep up with inflation (as measured by the CPI-W).

CHAPTER THREE

Spousal Social Security Benefits

Upon reaching age 62, even if you have no work history of your own, you can begin receiving a Social Security benefit as the spouse of somebody who is entitled to a retirement or disability benefit, if you meet one of three requirements:

1. You have been married to your spouse for at least one year,
2. You, together with your spouse, are the natural parent of a child, or
3. In the month before you married your current spouse, you were eligible to collect a widow(er) benefit or a spousal benefit based on another spouse's work record.

If you are not yet age 62, you can receive a spousal benefit if you meet the other applicable requirements and you have in your care a child who is entitled to child's benefits on your spouse's record (which we'll discuss in Chapter 6) and who is under age 16 or disabled.

It's important to note that you cannot claim spousal benefits until your spouse has filed for his/her own retirement benefit.

In addition, you cannot receive spousal Social Security benefits if you have filed for your own retirement benefit and your own primary insurance amount is greater than one-half of your spouse's primary insurance amount.

Filing for Spousal Benefits after Full Retirement Age

If you wait until full retirement age to begin collecting spousal benefits, and you are not receiving a retirement benefit, your spousal benefit will be equal to 50% of your spouse's primary insurance amount.[1] Unlike retirement benefits, spousal benefits are not increased by waiting beyond full retirement age to claim them.

EXAMPLE: Lydia's primary insurance amount is $1,800. If her husband Carl has no work record of

---

[1] As we'll discuss in Chapters 6 and 7, your spousal benefit could be reduced as a result of the family maximum if other people are also claiming benefits on your spouse's work record or as a result of the Government Pension Offset if you receive a pension.

his own and he claims spousal benefits at or after full retirement age, he would receive 50% of Lydia's PIA, or $900 per month.

Filing for Spousal Benefits prior to Full Retirement Age

If you claim spousal benefits prior to full retirement age, your spousal benefit will be reduced as a function of how many months early you claimed. The reduction will be $^{25}/_{36}$ of 1% for each month early, up to 36 months. For each month in excess of 36 months, the reduction is $^{5}/_{12}$ of 1%. Translate that into years, and you get the following table:

If you claim spousal benefits...	You will receive 50% of your spouse's PIA multiplied by:
At full retirement age	100%
1 year prior to FRA	91.67%
2 years prior to FRA	83.33%
3 years prior to FRA	75%
4 years prior to FRA	70%
5 years prior to FRA	65%

EXAMPLE: Nadia is not eligible for a retirement benefit of her own. Her husband Timothy has a primary insurance amount of $1,400. If Nadia claims her spousal benefit three years prior to reaching full retirement age, she will receive $525 per month, calculated as 75% of 50% of her husband's $1,400 PIA.

Spousal Benefits with Retirement Benefits

If you file for spousal benefits at the same time you are receiving a retirement benefit of your own, your spousal benefit will be calculated as follows[1]:

| Reduction factor, if applicable (from previous table) | x | 50% of your spouse's PIA, minus your PIA |

Your own retirement benefit will then be added to your spousal benefit to determine the total amount you'll receive.

EXAMPLE: Catherine's primary insurance amount is $700. Her husband Michael's primary insurance amount is $1,600. If Catherine files for spousal benefits and her own retirement benefit four years

---

[1] There are two exceptions to this calculation. First, in the event that this calculation would yield a negative result, you would simply receive your own retirement benefit and no spousal benefit (rather than receiving a negative spousal benefit). Second, if you filed for retirement benefits after reaching full retirement age (such that your monthly retirement benefit is greater than your PIA), then your monthly retirement benefit will be used in this calculation rather than your PIA.

prior to full retirement age, the total amount she will receive is $595, calculated as follows:

- Catherine's own retirement benefit of $525, calculated as $700 x 75% (due to claiming four years prior to FRA), plus
- Catherine's spousal benefit of $70, calculated as:

70% (from previous table)   x   [(50% x 1,600) − 700]

Deemed Filing

It's also important to know that if you are eligible for spousal benefits and for your own retirement benefit, and you file for either of the two prior to reaching full retirement age, you will be "deemed" to have filed for the other type of benefit as well. The purpose of this rule is to prevent you from being able to file for only one type of benefit, while allowing the other benefit to continue to grow.

If, however, you have reached full retirement age, you can file for just your spousal benefit by filing what's known as a "restricted application," thereby allowing your own retirement benefit to continue growing until age 70. We'll discuss this more thoroughly in Chapter 11.

EXAMPLE: Earl's full retirement age is 66. At age 64, he files for a spousal benefit on his wife's earnings record. As a result, he's deemed to have filed for his own retirement benefit as well.

If Earl had waited until age 66, he could file a "restricted application" for spousal benefits only. If he did so, his own retirement benefit could continue to grow until age 70.

2016 Changes to Deemed Filing Rules

As a result of the Bipartisan Budget Act of 2015, for anybody who was born after January 1, 1954, the deemed filing rules work somewhat differently. Specifically, deemed filing will apply even beyond full retirement age.

EXAMPLE: Betty was born in 1956. At age 68 (i.e., after reaching full retirement age), she files for spousal benefits on her husband's work record. Because she is subject to the new deemed filing rules, she will be deemed to have filed for her own retirement benefit as well.

In addition, deemed filing can occur simply as a result of becoming eligible for spousal or retirement benefits while receiving the other type of benefit.

EXAMPLE: Clarence was born in 1959. At age 62, he files for his own retirement benefit. Three years later, his wife files for her own retirement benefit, making Clarence eligible for a spousal benefit. He will automatically be deemed to have filed for a spousal benefit at that time.

Chapter 3 Simple Summary

- If you claim spousal benefits at (or after) full retirement age, your spousal benefit will be equal to 50% of your spouse's primary insurance amount—unless you are also entitled to a retirement benefit at that time, in which case your spousal benefit will usually be reduced by the amount of your PIA.

- If you claim spousal benefits prior to full retirement age, the amount you receive per month will be permanently reduced.

- In most cases, the youngest age at which you can qualify for spousal benefits is 62.

- If you are eligible for both spousal benefits and your own retirement benefit, and you claim either one prior to full retirement age, you will be "deemed" to have filed for the other benefit as well.

- If you were born after January 1, 1954, deemed filing will be applicable even beyond full retirement age.

CHAPTER FOUR

Widow(er) Social Security Benefits

If you are a widow or widower, you may be able to claim a widow(er) benefit based on your deceased spouse's work record. In most cases, in order to be eligible for widow(er) benefits:

- The marriage must have lasted at least nine months,
- You must be at least 60 years old (or disabled and at least age 50),
- You must not have remarried, unless you remarried *after* reaching age 60, and
- Your spouse must have been "fully insured" at the time of his/her death.[1]

---

[1] For exceptions to these general requirements, see section 404.335 of the Code of Federal Regulations, available at:
ssa.gov/OP_Home/cfr20/404/404-0335.htm

To be fully insured, your spouse must have earned a number of Social Security credits equal to his/her age at the time of death, minus 22, subject to two exceptions:

1. If your spouse died prior to age 28, six credits are required for fully insured status, and
2. No more than 40 credits are required, even if your spouse was older than 62 at the time of his/her death.

Calculation of Widow(er) Benefits

The amount of the widow(er) benefit will be 100% of the deceased spouse's primary insurance amount if:

- The deceased spouse was younger than full retirement age and had not yet filed for benefits, and
- The surviving spouse claims widow(er) benefits at or after his or her own full retirement age.

If the deceased spouse had claimed benefits earlier than FRA, the surviving spouse's widow(er) benefit, rather than being based on the deceased spouse's PIA, will be based on the *larger* of:

- The amount that the deceased spouse was receiving, or

- 82.5% of the deceased spouse's primary insurance amount.

EXAMPLE: Henry has a full retirement age of 67. He claims his retirement benefits at age 64, meaning his retirement benefit is 80% of his primary insurance amount.

Henry then dies at age 65. His wife Wanda (who has already reached full retirement age) claims a widow's benefit immediately. Wanda's widow's benefit will be 82.5% of Henry's PIA (because she gets the greater of 82.5% or the amount he was receiving, which was 80%).

If the deceased spouse claimed benefits after reaching FRA, the surviving spouse's widow(er) benefit will be based on the amount that the deceased spouse was receiving.

EXAMPLE: Harry claims benefits at age 68, then dies at age 69. Harry's wife Rita (who has already reached full retirement age) claims a widow's benefit immediately. Rita's widow's benefit will be equal to the benefit that Harry had been receiving at the time of his death (which will be greater than Harry's primary insurance amount, because he claimed after full retirement age).

If the deceased spouse had reached full retirement age but had not yet filed for benefits, the surviving spouse's widow(er) benefit will be based on the amount that the deceased spouse would have received if he/she had filed on the date of his/her death.

EXAMPLE: Lynn dies at age 69, having never filed for her own retirement benefit. Lynn's husband Hank (who has already reached full retirement age) immediately claims a widower's benefit. Hank's widower's benefit will be equal to the amount that Lynn would have received if she had filed for her own benefit on her date of death.

Like retirement benefits and spousal benefits, widow(er) benefits are adjusted for inflation. This inflation adjustment includes any time between the date at which the first spouse dies and the date at which the surviving spouse claims a widow(er)'s benefit.

EXAMPLE: Wendy files for retirement benefits at age 65, then dies at 67. Her husband Howard is 60 years old at the time of Wendy's death. Six years later, at his full retirement age, Howard files for widower benefits. He'll receive the amount that Wendy was receiving, adjusted for any inflation that occurred over the six intervening years.

Claiming Widow(er) Benefits Prior to Full Retirement Age

If the surviving spouse claims widow(er) benefits *prior* to reaching full retirement age, the amount received will be reduced. Widow(er) benefits claimed at age 60 (the minimum age for widow(er) benefits) will be equal to 71.5% of the amount that would have been received if claimed at full retirement age.[1]

EXAMPLE: June dies at age 63, having never filed for benefits. As discussed previously, this means that if her husband Frank claims his widower's benefit at full retirement age, he will receive an amount equal to June's primary insurance amount. If Frank claims at age 60, however, he will only receive 71.5% of June's primary insurance amount.

The reduction in widow(er) benefits decreases proportionately as the claimant nears full retirement age. So, for example, if the surviving spouse claims widower benefits halfway between age 60 and full retirement age, the amount received will be 85.75% (that is, halfway between 71.5% and 100%) of the amount that would have been received at FRA.

---

[1] Exception: If the deceased spouse had claimed retirement benefits prior to FRA and the surviving spouse claims widow(er) benefits prior to FRA as well, the widow(er) benefit will be greater than what the above would indicate. See Appendix A for details.

Full Retirement Age for Widow(er) Benefits

You may have a slightly different full retirement age for the purpose of calculating widow(er) benefits than you do for the purpose of calculating retirement benefits or spousal benefits. As compared to the FRA chart for retirement benefits (as shown in Chapter 2), the FRA chart for survivor benefits has each of the dates of birth shifted two years into the future, as follows:

Year of Birth[1]	Full Retirement Age for Widow(er) Benefits
1939 or earlier	65
1940	65 and 2 months
1941	65 and 4 months
1942	65 and 6 months
1943	65 and 8 months
1944	65 and 10 months
1945-1956	66
1957	66 and 2 months
1958	66 and 4 months
1959	66 and 6 months
1960	66 and 8 months
1961	66 and 10 months
1962 or later	67

---

[1] As with retirement benefits, if your birthday is January 1st, you will be treated as if you were born in the prior year for the purpose of determining your FRA.

Widow(er) Benefits Combined with Other Benefits

If a person claims widow(er) benefits at the same time that he/she is receiving a retirement benefit (or a spousal benefit) the total amount he/she receives will be the greater of the two benefit amounts.[1]

Chapter 4 Simple Summary

- If you are a widow(er) and your spouse had earned a sufficient number of Social Security credits by the time of his/her death, you may be eligible for a widow(er) benefit.

- Age 60 is usually the earliest date at which a person can claim widow(er) benefits.

- The amount of the widow(er) benefit you receive depends both on the date at which your deceased spouse began claiming benefits and on the date at which you begin claiming your widow(er) benefit.

---

[1] Technically, if your widow(er) benefit is greater than your retirement benefit, you receive your retirement benefit, plus your widow(er) benefit, after reducing your widow(er) benefit by the amount of your retirement benefit.

PART TWO

Rules for Less Common Situations

CHAPTER FIVE

Social Security for Divorced Spouses

There are two types of benefits that can be claimed based on an ex-spouse's earnings record:

1. Divorced spouse benefits, and
2. Surviving divorced spouse benefits.

The rules for both types of benefits are quite similar to those for still-married couples.

Qualifying for Divorced Spouse Benefits

To qualify for spousal benefits based on an ex-spouse's earnings record:

- The marriage must have lasted at least ten years,

- You must be age 62 or older, and
- You must not currently be married.[1]

In addition, either a) your ex-spouse must have already claimed his/her own retirement (or disability) benefit, or b) he/she must be eligible to claim such a benefit and you have been divorced for at least two years.

For the most part, divorced spouse benefits are calculated the same way as regular spousal benefits. That is, if you claim at full retirement age, your benefit as an ex-spouse will be equal to:

- 50% of your ex-spouse's primary insurance amount, minus
- The larger of your monthly retirement benefit or your PIA (if you are receiving a retirement benefit).

Also, like regular spousal benefits:

- If you claim prior to your FRA, your divorced spouse benefit will be reduced,
- You do not get any additional benefit for waiting beyond full retirement age, and

---

[1] There is one exception. If you are receiving benefits as a divorced spouse, and you marry somebody who is receiving benefits on somebody else's work record, you can continue receiving benefits on your prior spouse's work record. See CFR 404.332 for more information: ssa.gov/OP_Home/cfr20/404/404-0332.htm

- You cannot claim divorced spouse benefits if you have filed for your own retirement benefit and your own primary insurance amount is greater than one-half of your ex-spouse's primary insurance amount.

As with normal spousal benefits, if you claim divorced spouse benefits prior to full retirement age, you will be deemed to have filed for your own retirement benefit as well. (And conversely, if you file for your own retirement benefit prior to full retirement age, you will be deemed to have filed for your divorced spousal benefit as well.)

If, however, you wait until full retirement age to claim divorced spouse benefits, it will not be treated as filing for your own benefit—thereby allowing you to receive divorced spouse benefits for a few years while you allow your own retirement benefit to grow until age 70.[1] (We'll discuss this strategy more thoroughly in Chapter 11.)

---

[1] As mentioned in Chapter 3, however, as a result of the Bipartisan Budget Act of 2015, this option to file for spousal-only while allowing your own retirement benefit to continue growing will not be available to anybody who was born after January 1, 1954.

Qualifying for Surviving Divorced Spouse Benefits

If your ex-spouse has passed away, you may be eligible for surviving divorced spouse benefits on his or her work record. In order to qualify:

- The marriage must have lasted at least ten years,
- You must be age 60 or older (or disabled and at least age 50),
- You must not currently be married (or you remarried after reaching age 60), and
- Your ex-spouse must have been "fully insured" (as explained in Chapter 4) at the time of his/her death.

Calculating Benefits for a Surviving Divorced Spouse

In general, surviving divorced spouse benefits are calculated the same way as widow(er) benefits. That is, assuming you have reached full retirement age by the time you claim surviving divorced spouse benefits:

- If your ex-spouse died prior to full retirement age without having filed for retirement benefits, your widow(er) benefit will be

100% of your deceased ex-spouse's primary insurance amount.

- If your ex-spouse died after reaching full retirement age without having filed for retirement benefits, your widow(er) benefit will be equal to the amount your deceased ex-spouse would have received if he/she had filed on the date of death.

- If your ex-spouse was already claiming benefits by the time of death, your widow(er) benefit will be equal to the greater of a) the amount your deceased ex-spouse was receiving prior to death or b) 82.5% of your deceased ex-spouse's primary insurance amount.

If you claim surviving divorced spouse benefits prior to FRA, the benefit you receive will be reduced.

And as with regular widow(er) benefits, if you claim surviving divorced spouse benefits at the same time that you're receiving a retirement benefit, the total amount you receive will be the greater of the two benefit amounts.[1]

---

[1] Again, technically, if the widow(er) benefit is greater than your own retirement benefit, you receive your own retirement benefit, plus the widow(er) benefit, after reducing the widow(er) benefit by the amount of your own retirement benefit.

If You've Remarried

If you remarry (or remarry before age 60 in the case of widow(er) benefits), you will usually not be eligible for benefits on your prior spouse's record, unless your new spouse dies or you get divorced (that is, divorced from your second spouse), in which case you will again be eligible for benefits on your first spouse's record. If your second marriage also lasted ten years, you can claim benefits on the work record of either ex-spouse.

EXAMPLE: Anne is married to Bob for 15 years. Then they get divorced, and Anne marries Christopher. After 15 years of marriage to Christopher, they too get divorced. When Anne reaches age 62, she can claim spousal benefits on the work record of either ex-spouse. Because Bob made more than Christopher over the course of his career, Anne chooses to claim spousal benefits on Bob's record.

    A few years later, Christopher dies. Anne is now eligible for surviving divorced spouse benefits on his work record. Despite Christopher's lower earnings, surviving divorced spouse benefits on his record are greater than divorced spouse benefits on Bob's record (because divorced spouse benefits are based on 50% of the ex-spouse's benefit, whereas surviving divorced spouse benefits are based on 100% of the deceased ex-spouse's benefit). So Anne switches to claiming surviving divorced spouse benefits on Christopher's record.

A few years later, Bob dies too. Anne can now switch to receiving surviving divorced spouse benefits on Bob's record (which, because of Bob's higher earnings, should be greater than the surviving divorced spouse benefits on Christopher's record that Anne had been receiving).

Chapter 5 Simple Summary

- The eligibility requirements for divorced spouse benefits are similar to the requirements for spousal benefits for still-married couples, with the notable exception that the marriage must have lasted at least 10 years. (Ditto for the eligibility requirements for surviving divorced spouse benefits.)

- For the most part, benefits based on the work record of an ex-spouse are calculated the same way as benefits based on the work record of a current spouse.

- After a divorce, if you marry somebody else, you will usually not be eligible for spousal benefits based on the work record of your first spouse (unless your second spouse dies or you get divorced). Similarly, remarriage prior to age 60 will usually make you ineligible for widow(er) benefits on your ex-spouse's work record.

CHAPTER SIX

Child Benefits

The children of people who are receiving retirement (or disability) benefits, as well as the children of people who have died, may be eligible for a Social Security benefit of their own. To be eligible for such benefits, a child must:

1. Be a dependent of the worker in question,[1]
2. Be the child, legally adopted child, or stepchild of the worker,[2]
3. Be unmarried, and
4. Be under age 18 or be disabled with a disability that began before age 22.[3]

---

[1] The definition of "dependent" in this context is not the same definition that's used for tax purposes. See Code of Federal Regulations sections 404.360-404.365: ssa.gov/OP_Home/cfr20/404/404-0000.htm

[2] Grandchildren and step-grandchildren can also qualify if the child's parents are deceased or disabled and the other requirements are met.

[3] A full-time student in grade 12 or below can receive benefits until they are 19.

Calculating Children's Benefits

In the case of children qualifying for benefits based on the earnings record of a retired or disabled worker, the amount of the child's benefit is 50% of the worker's primary insurance amount. For children of deceased workers, the child's benefit is 75% of the deceased worker's primary insurance amount. In either case, however, the amount the child actually receives could be reduced as a result of the family maximum.

Family Maximum

There is a maximum amount that a family can receive based on the work record of a given person. That maximum ranges from 150% to 187% of the person's primary insurance amount. For a person becoming eligible for benefits in 2019, the maximum is calculated as:

- 150% of the first $1,184 of the worker's PIA, plus
- 272% of the worker's PIA from $1,184 to $1,708, plus
- 134% of the worker's PIA from $1,708 to $2,228, plus
- 175% of the worker's PIA over $2,228.

When the amount that a family would ordinarily receive (prior to considering the maximum) exceeds the maximum calculated based on that person's PIA, the benefits of each person other than the worker are reduced proportionately to keep the total amount the family receives under the maximum.

EXAMPLE: John and Claire are married, both age 62, with two legally adopted young children. John's primary insurance amount is $1,800. The family maximum benefit based on his work record (calculated using the rules on the previous page) is $3,324. Claire's work history is not sufficient for her to receive a retirement benefit of her own.

If John claims his own benefit at his full retirement age, and Claire claims her spousal benefit at her full retirement age, the members of John's family would be eligible for the following benefits (prior to considering the family maximum):

- John: $1,800
- Claire: $900
- Child 1: $900
- Child 2: $900

The total of those four benefits is $4,500, which exceeds the $3,324 family maximum based on John's PIA. As a result, the benefits received by Claire and the two children will be reduced proportionately until the family's total benefit is under the maximum. In the end, John will receive $1,800, and the other three will each receive $508.

It's important to note that the formula uses the worker's primary insurance amount rather than the monthly benefit he/she is actually receiving. So even if John had claimed his retirement benefit before or after full retirement age, such that he was receiving an amount smaller or larger than his primary insurance amount, the amounts that Claire and the kids receive would not change.

Also of note: If Claire was *not* receiving a spousal benefit, and was instead receiving a retirement benefit based on her own work record, her benefit would not count toward the family maximum. (As mentioned above, the family maximum is only the maximum that can be received with regard to one particular worker's work record.) As a result, each of the two children would be able to receive a larger benefit.

Important note: Benefits as a divorced spouse or surviving divorced spouse will not be reduced due to the family maximum. Nor, in turn, will the benefits of an ex-spouse be counted toward the maximum benefit for the rest of the family.

Effect of Children on Spousal Benefits

In addition to qualifying for benefits themselves, children can make a parent eligible for benefits when they would not otherwise be eligible. Specifically, if you meet all of the requirements to collect spousal benefits aside from the fact that you are not yet 62 years old, you can still qualify for benefits if you have in your care a child who is under 16 or disabled and who is entitled to child's benefits on your spouse's work record.

Chapter 6 Simple Summary

- If they are under age 18 or disabled, children of people receiving retirement or disability benefits may be eligible for a benefit of up to 50% of the worker's primary insurance amount.

- If they are under age 18 or disabled, children of people who have died may be eligible for a benefit of up to 75% of the deceased parent's primary insurance amount.

- There is a maximum benefit that can be paid to a family (not including divorced spouses) based on the work record of a single person. That benefit can range from 150% to 187% of the worker's primary insurance amount.

- In the event that a family would exceed the maximum benefit, the benefits of each person other than the worker will be reduced proportionately until the total amount the family receives is below the maximum.

CHAPTER SEVEN

Social Security with a Pension

If you receive a pension from a job for which you did not have to pay Social Security taxes (e.g., work as a government employee), any Social Security benefits you would otherwise be eligible to receive could be reduced by two special rules:

1. The Windfall Elimination Provision (WEP), or
2. The Government Pension Offset (GPO).

Note that neither of these rules applies in the case of a worker who receives a pension from work that was subject to Social Security taxes.

Windfall Elimination Provision

If you receive a pension from a job for which you did not have to pay Social Security taxes, the

Windfall Elimination Provision (WEP) will result in you receiving a smaller Social Security benefit for any other work that you did—that is, work that *was* covered by Social Security taxes.

EXAMPLE: Elena works for 21 years as a police officer—a job in which she does not pay Social Security taxes. She then works another 19 years at a private security firm. Because of her work for the local government, Elena qualifies for a pension. And because of her work for the security firm, she also qualifies for Social Security. The Windfall Elimination Provision will reduce the amount of Social Security benefits that Elena receives.

The Windfall Elimination Provision works by changing the formula used to calculate your primary insurance amount.[1] From there, any percentage adjustments are applied as normal for claiming earlier or later than full retirement age.

As discussed in Chapter 2, for people not affected by the WEP, Social Security replaces a certain percentage of their AIME (i.e., their average monthly earnings from their 35 highest-earning

---

[1] Because it changes your primary insurance amount, the WEP also affects the amount(s) your spouse or children can receive based on your work record. However, upon your death, your PIA is recalculated without the effect of the WEP. In other words, the WEP will not affect the amount of *survivor* benefits your spouse or children could receive.

years, after adjusting those earnings for wage inflation). For somebody becoming eligible for Social Security in 2019, if claimed at full retirement age, Social Security would replace:

- 90% of AIME up to $926, plus
- 32% of AIME from $926 to $5,583, plus
- 15% of AIME beyond $5,583.[1]

The Windfall Elimination Provision changes the 90% in the first line of the calculation to a lower number, depending on the number of years in which you had "substantial earnings" covered by Social Security taxes. (The "substantial earnings" threshold changes by year. For 2019, it's $24,675.)

- If you have 20 or fewer years with substantial earnings, the figure used will be 40% instead of 90%.
- For each year of substantial earnings beyond 20, the figure increases by 5% (until you reach the original 90% figure).

Important exception: The Windfall Elimination Provision will never reduce your primary insurance amount by more than 50% of your monthly pension amount. (If you are paid a pension in the form of a lump sum, the pension will be recalculated as if it were paid monthly.)

---

[1] Note that earnings from work not subject to Social Security tax would not be included in this calculation.

Government Pension Offset

If you receive a pension from work you did for a federal, state, or local government agency, and you did not have to pay Social Security taxes on your earnings from that work, the Government Pension Offset (GPO) reduces any Social Security spousal or survivor benefits you would receive based on your spouse's work record. The reduction in monthly benefits is calculated as $2/3$ of the monthly pension amount you receive. (Again, in the case of a pension taken as a lump sum, the reduction will be calculated as if the pension had been paid out on a monthly basis.)

EXAMPLE: Bob worked for many years in an administrative role for his local fire department. Bob's job was not subject to Social Security taxes. Upon his retirement at age 67, Bob gets a monthly pension of $2,100 per month. At her full retirement age, Bob's wife Janice begins claiming her Social Security benefit of $2,000 per month.

Ordinarily, this would mean that Bob could get a spousal Social Security benefit of $1,000 per month (50% of Janice's PIA) as long as he claims it at full retirement age or later. However, because of the Government Pension Offset, Bob's monthly spousal benefit will be reduced by $1,400 ($2/3$ of his $2,100 monthly pension), thereby eliminating it completely.

Upon Janice's death, Bob will be able to claim a Social Security survivor benefit on Janice's record. Ordinarily, since Janice claimed her benefit at her full retirement age and because Bob is claiming the survivor benefit after full retirement age, he'd be able to get the $2,000 per month that she was receiving. But, again, the GPO will reduce the benefit by $1,400, thereby leaving him with a monthly survivor benefit of $600.

Chapter 7 Simple Summary

- If you receive a pension from work you did that was not covered by Social Security taxes, the Windfall Elimination Provision (WEP) will reduce the Social Security benefits you (and your spouse or children, if applicable) can receive from any work you did that *was* covered by Social Security taxes.

- The degree to which your retirement benefit is reduced by the WEP depends on how many years you had "substantial earnings" that were covered by Social Security taxes.

- If you receive a pension from government work you did that was not covered by Social Security taxes, the Government Pension Offset will reduce any spousal or widow(er) Social Security benefits you could receive by $2/3$ of the amount of your monthly pension.

CHAPTER EIGHT

The Earnings Test

If your retirement plan includes a stage of semi-retirement, you'll want to take the Social Security earnings test into consideration when making your plans.

In brief, the earnings test says that, for years before full retirement age during which you work while claiming your own retirement benefit, for every $2 by which your annual earnings exceed a certain amount ($17,640 in 2019), your Social Security benefit for that year will be reduced by $1.

EXAMPLE: Neal is two years away from full retirement age and is already claiming Social Security benefits. He worked this year and earned $25,000 (or $7,360 in excess of $17,640). As a result of the earnings test, his annual benefit will be reduced by $3,680 (half of the $7,360 excess).

There are four additional points worth noting here.

First, due to the "grace year" rule, which we'll discuss later in this chapter, it's likely that the earnings test will not reduce the amount you receive in your first year of retirement, even if you earn more than the annual threshold amount.

Second, after reaching full retirement age, the earnings test doesn't apply. You can earn as much as you want without a reduction in your benefits.

Third, for earnings test purposes, only wages, earnings from self-employment, and a few less-common types of income are considered. (For example, pension income, IRA distributions, interest income, and capital gains do *not* count.)[1]

Fourth, the calculation is different for the year in which you reach full retirement age. In that year:

- The exempt amount is higher ($46,920 for someone reaching FRA in 2019),
- $1 of benefits is withheld for every $3 of earnings in excess of the exempt amount rather than $1 being withheld for every $2 of excess earnings, and
- Earnings for months of the year after you reach FRA are not taken into consideration.

---

[1] For a full list of types of income that would be included for earnings test purposes, see Section 1811 of the Social Security Handbook:
ssa.gov/OP_Home/handbook/handbook.18/handbook-1811.html

How the Reduction Is Applied

Contrary to what you might expect, if your benefits are reduced as a result of the earnings test, they will not be reduced on a pro-rata basis throughout the year. Rather, your benefits will be withheld completely until the withholding requirement for the year has been satisfied.[1]

EXAMPLE: Aside from the earnings test, Laurie's Social Security benefit would be $18,000 per year ($1,500 per month). However, because of the test, her benefit will be reduced by $4,500 this year. As a result, Laurie will receive no benefits for January, February, or March. Then she will receive full benefits for the remaining nine months of the year.

---

[1] When you initially claim Social Security benefits, the SSA employee with whom you speak should ask you to estimate your annual earnings for that year and the following year. This information will be used to determine how much of your benefits to withhold. If at any point during the year it becomes clear that you will earn significantly more or less than you had estimated, you can call the SSA to let them know to adjust your withholdings. At the end of each year, you will "settle up" with the SSA based on your actual earnings.

Adjustment Upon Reaching FRA

When you reach full retirement age, your benefits will be recalculated to adjust for the months in which, as a result of the earnings test, you did not actually receive full benefits. For example, if you claimed benefits 48 months before FRA, but the earnings test eliminated or reduced your benefits for 12 of those 48 months, your monthly benefit will be recalculated (i.e., increased) as if you had only claimed 36 months early rather than 48.[1]

Earnings Test for Spousal, Survivor, and Child Benefits

In the event that other family members are entitled to benefits based on your work record (e.g., spousal benefits or child benefits), the earnings test will reduce their benefits as well as yours if your earnings exceed the applicable threshold.

EXAMPLE: Prior to considering the earnings test, Wesley is entitled to a retirement benefit of $1,000

---

[1] While the adjustment is effective as of full retirement age, it is often several months (or even up to a year) before the adjustment is actually processed. As a result, the first monthly check that reflects the adjustment will also include a lump sum for the months (going back to the month in which you reached full retirement age) that should have been increased.

per month, and his wife Donna is entitled to a spousal benefit of $500 per month. However, Wesley is younger than full retirement age, and his annual earnings for the year are $30,000. As a result, the earnings test will reduce the family's total benefit for the year by $6,180 (half of the excess of $30,000 over $17,640).

Wesley and Donna's $1,500 total monthly benefit will be withheld entirely until the necessary $6,180 has been withheld. As a result, they will receive no benefits for the months of January, February, March, April, or May.

By that point, however, their benefits will have been reduced by $7,500, which is more than the necessary $6,180. In the following January, they will receive back the excess withholding (of $1,320) from May. Because Wesley's benefit makes up two-thirds of their total monthly benefit, two-thirds of the $1,320 will be paid to Wesley, and the remaining one-third will be paid to Donna.

If somebody *else* (e.g., your spouse or widow/widower) is working while receiving benefits based on your work record, the earnings test could reduce that person's benefits (but not your own).

EXAMPLE: Prior to considering the earnings test, Wesley is entitled to a retirement benefit of $1,000 per month, and his wife Donna is entitled to a spousal benefit of $500 per month.

However, Donna is younger than full retirement age, and her annual earnings for the year are $30,000. (This time we're assuming that Wesley is retired.) In this case, the earnings test will reduce *Donna's* benefit for the year by $6,180 (half of the excess of $30,000 over $17,640). Wesley's retirement benefit will not be affected. Because Donna's benefit prior to considering the earnings test is only $6,000 per year ($500 x 12), it will be eliminated completely for this year.

Earnings Test during First Year of Retirement

If you retire in the middle of the year, it's possible that the earnings test will not affect your benefits for the remainder of the year, even if by the date of your retirement you have already earned an amount greater than the annual threshold.

In Social Security jargon, the earnings test will not result in reduced benefits for any "non-service month in a grace year." A "non-service month" is a month in which you earn less than $1/12$th of the annual threshold for the earnings test (so, $1,470 for 2019) or in which you do not perform substantial services for your business if you are self-employed.[1] And the first year in which you have a non-

---

[1] Performing "substantial services" for your business usually means working more than 45 hours over the course of the month. It is possible, however, that working as few as 15 hours can be considered substantial services if you manage a large business or you work in a highly skilled occupation.

service month while claiming a retirement benefit, spousal benefit, or widow(er) benefit is called your "grace year."

EXAMPLE: Beverly retired at age 63 on October 1, after earning $80,000 in the first nine months of the year. She claims her retirement benefit immediately, and she does not work for the rest of the year.

Because Beverly is not working October through December, each of those months will be considered "non-service months." And because this is the first year in which she has a non-service month in which she is also claiming a retirement benefit, this year will be considered her "grace year." Therefore, despite the fact that Beverly earned well above the annual threshold amount for the earnings test, the earnings test will not reduce the benefits she receives in October, November, or December, because those months are considered non-service months in a grace year.

Chapter 8 Simple Summary

- Prior to full retirement age, if you work while collecting retirement benefits, the total amount your family receives based on your work record will be reduced by 50% of the amount by which your annual earnings exceed a certain threshold ($17,640 for 2019).

- If a family member is working while receiving a benefit based on your work record, their benefit (but not your own benefit) will be reduced if their earnings exceed the same threshold mentioned above.

- The earnings test does not apply after you reach full retirement age. And in the year in which you reach full retirement age, the reduction in benefits is smaller for a given level of earnings than it would be in prior years.

- Once you reach full retirement age, your benefit will be recalculated to account for months in which your benefit was reduced or eliminated as a result of the earnings test.

PART THREE

Social Security Planning: When to Claim Benefits

CHAPTER NINE

When to Claim Benefits: Unmarried Retirees

Even if you are married, the place to start when trying to figure out when to claim Social Security is with a solid understanding of the (less complicated) analysis for unmarried retirees.

And before we go any further, let's make sure we're on the same page about an important point: The decision of when to retire is separate from the decision of when to claim Social Security benefits. For example, depending on circumstances, you might find that it makes sense to retire at a given age, yet hold off on claiming Social Security until a later date—maybe even several years later.

As we've discussed, the earlier you claim Social Security, the less you'll receive per month. For example, the following table (reproduced from Chapter 2) shows how retirement benefits are affected by the age at which you first claim them:

Age when you claim retirement benefits	Amount of retirement benefit
5 years before FRA	70% of PIA
4 years before FRA	75% of PIA
3 years before FRA	80% of PIA
2 years before FRA	86.67% of PIA
1 year before FRA	93.33% of PIA
at FRA	100% of PIA
1 year after FRA	108% of PIA
2 years after FRA	116% of PIA
3 years after FRA	124% of PIA
4 years after FRA	132% of PIA

In other words, by waiting until age 70 rather than claiming as early as possible at age 62, you can increase your monthly benefit amount by roughly three-quarters. Of course, by waiting, you decrease the *number* of months in which you'll be receiving a Social Security check.

So how can you tell if the trade-off is worth it? One way to compare two possible ages for claiming benefits is to compute the age to which you would have to live for one strategy to become superior to the other strategy. Another way to analyze the decision is to compare the payout you get from delaying Social Security to the level of income you can safely get from other retirement income sources.

Computing the Breakeven Point

EXAMPLE: Alex and Bob are both retired and unmarried. Both are age 62, both have a full retirement age of 66 and 6 months, and both have exactly the same earnings history. In fact, the only difference between the two is that Alex claims his retirement benefit at age 62, while Bob waits all the way until 70. Even though Alex claims benefits at age 62, he doesn't need the money right now, so he keeps it in his savings account, where it earns a return that precisely matches inflation.

By age 70, because he has been receiving benefits for eight years, Alex is far better off than Bob. However, starting at age 70, Bob starts to catch up (because he's receiving a monthly benefit equal to 128% of his primary insurance amount, while Alex is receiving a monthly benefit equal to 72.5% of his primary insurance amount).

In the end, Bob's cumulative benefit surpasses Alex's cumulative benefit halfway through age 80. From age 80.5 onward, Bob's lead over Alex continues to grow.

The takeaway: For an unmarried retiree, from a breakeven perspective, if you live past age 80.5, you will have been better off waiting until age 70 instead of claiming as early as possible at age 62.[1]

---

[1] While this example assumes a full retirement age of 66 and 6 months, the breakeven point for people with an FRA of 67 is not meaningfully different. (Specifically, it occurs one month earlier.)

According to the Social Security Administration, the average total life expectancy for a 62-year-old female is 84.8. For a male, it's 82.[1] In other words, from a breakeven perspective, most unmarried retirees will be best served by waiting to take their retirement benefit.

Comparing Social Security to Other Income Options

When you delay Social Security, you give up a certain amount of money right now (i.e., this month's or this year's benefits) in exchange for a stream of payments that will increase with inflation for the rest of your life.

Take, for example, somebody with a full retirement age of 66. If her benefit at full retirement age would be $1,000 per month, her benefit at age 62 would be $750 per month, and at age 63 it would be $800 per month.

Therefore, waiting from age 62 to age 63 is the equivalent of paying $9,000 (that is, $750 forgone per month, for 12 months) in exchange for a source of income that pays $600 per year (that is, a $50 increase in monthly retirement benefit, times 12 months per year), adjusted for inflation, for the rest of her life.

---

[1] From the life expectancy table available at: ssa.gov/oact/STATS/table4c6.html

Dividing $600 by $9,000 shows us that de-laying Social Security retirement benefits from age 62 to 63 provides a 6.67% payout. Let's see how that compares to other sources of retirement income.

Inflation-adjusted single premium immedi-ate lifetime annuities are essentially pensions that you can purchase from an insurance company. With such an annuity, you pay the insurance com-pany an initial lump-sum (the premium for the pol-icy), and they promise to pay you a certain amount of income, adjusted for inflation, for the rest of your life. In other words, such annuities are a source of income *very* similar to Social Security.

As of this writing, according to the website immediateannuities.com (which provides annuity quotes from multiple insurance companies), the highest payout available to a 63-year-old female on such an annuity is 4.04%. For a male, the highest available payout would be 4.33%.[1] As you can see, both of these figures fall well short of the 6.67% payout that comes from delaying Social Security from 62 to 63.

Alternatively, we can compare the payout from delaying Social Security to the income that you can safely draw from a typical portfolio of stocks and bonds. Several studies have shown that, histor-ically in the U.S., retirees trying to fund a 30-year retirement run a significant risk of running out of money when they use initial inflation-adjusted

---

[1] Unfortunately, as of this writing, only one insurer is of-fering inflation-adjusted lifetime annuities.

withdrawal rates greater than 4%.[1] And it's worth noting that even a 4% withdrawal rate isn't a sure bet going forward, given that the studies show 4% to be *mostly* safe in the *past*, which is a far cry from *completely* safe in the *future*.

In other words, for each dollar of Social Security you give up now (by delaying benefits), you can expect to receive a greater level of income in the future than you could safely take from a dollar invested in a typical stock/bond portfolio.

A similar analysis can be performed for each year up to age 70, and the conclusion is the same: Delaying Social Security benefits can be an excellent way to increase the amount of income you can safely take from your portfolio.

EXAMPLE: Daniel is retired at 62 years old. His full retirement age is 66 and 6 months. He has $50,000 of annual expenses and a $600,000 portfolio. He is trying to decide between claiming benefits as early as possible at age 62 or spending down his portfolio while he waits to claim benefits until age 70.

Daniel's primary insurance amount (the amount he'd receive per month if he claimed his retirement benefit at full retirement age) is $2,500, which means he would receive:

---

[1] The most famous such study is the so-called "Trinity Study" by three professors (Cooley, Hubbard, and Walz) at Trinity University. In case you want to look it up, the actual title of the study is "Retirement Savings: Choosing a Withdrawal Rate That Is Sustainable."

- $1,812 per month ($21,744 per year) if he claimed benefits at age 62, or
- $3,200 per month ($38,400 per year) if he claimed benefits at age 70.

If Daniel claims his retirement benefit at age 62, he'll have to satisfy $28,256 of expenses every year from his portfolio (because Social Security will only be satisfying $21,744 out of $50,000). That is, he'll be using a 4.71% withdrawal rate ($28,256 divided by his $600,000 portfolio) starting at age 62. That's a higher withdrawal rate than many experts would recommend.

Alternatively, if Daniel delays Social Security until 70, he'll have to satisfy expenses of $11,600 each year (i.e., $50,000, minus $38,400 in Social Security benefits), plus an additional $38,400 for each of the eight years until he claims Social Security.

If Daniel allocates $307,200 (that is, $38,400 x 8) of his $600,000 portfolio to cash or something else very low-risk (in order to satisfy the additional expenses for those eight years), that leaves him with a typical stock/bond portfolio of $292,800. With a portfolio of $292,800 Daniel can satisfy his remaining $11,600 of annual expenses using a withdrawal rate of just 3.96%.

In effect, Daniel is spending down a portion of his portfolio in order to purchase additional Social Security benefits in the amount of $16,656 per year, starting at age 70. By doing so, he's reduced the withdrawal rate that he'll need to use from his portfolio for the remainder of his life, thereby reducing the probability that he'll run out of money. In addition, if Daniel's portfolio performs very poorly and he *does* run out of money, he'll be much better off in the wait-until-70 scenario than in the claim-at-62 scenario, because he'll be left with $38,400 of Social Security per year rather than $21,744.

Reasons Not to Delay Social Security

Of course, there are circumstances in which it would *not* make sense for an unmarried person to delay taking Social Security.

First and most obviously, if your finances are such that you absolutely *need* the income right now, then you have little choice in the matter.

Second, if you have reason to think that your life expectancy is well below average, it may be advantageous to claim benefits early. For example, if you have a medical condition such that you don't expect to make it past age 64, it would obviously not make a great deal of sense to choose to wait until age 70 to claim benefits.

Third, the higher market interest rates are, the less attractive it is to delay Social Security. For example, if inflation-adjusted interest rates (such as those on inflation-protected Treasury bonds known as TIPS) were 2-3% higher than they are as of this writing, the payout from inflation-adjusted lifetime annuities might be *higher* than the payout from delaying Social Security.

Chapter 9 Simple Summary

- For unmarried retirees, from a breakeven perspective, you'll be better served by claiming benefits at age 70 rather than at 62 if you expect to live past age 80.5. (And, for reference, the average total life expectancy for a 62-year-old female is 84.8. For a male, it's 82.)

- For unmarried retirees, on a dollar-for-dollar basis, the lifetime income you gain from delaying Social Security is generally greater than the level of income you can safely get from other sources. As a result, delaying Social Security can be a great way to increase the amount you can safely spend per year. (Or, said differently, it can be a great way to reduce the likelihood that you will outlive your money.)

- The shorter your life expectancy and the greater the available yield on inflation-protected bonds, the less desirable it is to delay claiming Social Security benefits.

CHAPTER TEN

When to Claim Benefits: Married Couples

As is the case for an unmarried person, the when-to-claim decision for married people depends largely on life expectancies. But in this case, *each* spouse's decision depends on *both* spouses' life expectancies.

When Should the High-PIA Spouse Claim Benefits?

As we discussed in the previous chapter, delaying Social Security is akin to buying an inflation-adjusted lifetime annuity—one that's a heck of a deal for many investors because it comes with a significantly higher payout and lower credit risk than annuities you can buy in the private marketplace.

In most cases, for the spouse in a married couple who has the higher of the two primary insurance amounts, delaying Social Security is just like that, but better. In addition to an unusually high payout and unusually low credit risk, the annuity now comes with the possibility of a survivor benefit as well.

EXAMPLE: Allan and Liz are married, both age 62. Liz's career earnings are rather low, because she spent many years out of the paid workforce doing volunteer work and caring for their children. As a result, Allan's primary insurance amount is much larger than Liz's.

After either Allan or Liz dies, the surviving spouse will be receiving an amount equal to Allan's benefit. (If Liz is the surviving spouse, it will be partially in the form of a widow's benefit.) As a result, if Allan chooses to hold off on claiming his own retirement benefit, he increases not only his own benefit while he's alive, but also Liz's widow's benefit in the event that he predeceases her.

In short, the decision for the higher-earning spouse includes the same considerations as for an unmarried retiree, with one major modification: The life expectancy in question is no longer just the person's own life expectancy, but rather the joint life expectancy of the two spouses (because delaying benefits will increase the amount paid out as long as *either* spouse is alive).

In other words, from a breakeven perspective, for it to be advantageous for the higher-earning spouse to delay his/her retirement benefit, only *one* spouse needs to make it to the breakeven point. As you can imagine, this often means that it's a very good deal for the high-PIA spouse to wait until age 70 to claim retirement benefits.

When Should the Low-PIA Spouse Claim Benefits?

For the spouse with the lower primary insurance amount, the decision of when to claim benefits works in much the same way as the decision for an unmarried person, but with one major modification: It's somewhat *less* advantageous for the low-PIA spouse to delay benefits, because doing so only increases the amount the couple will receive while they're *both* still alive.[1]

For example, if we look back at Allan and Liz from above, having Liz hold off on claiming Social Security does not increase the amount Allan will receive at any point. And it only increases the amount Liz will receive while Allan is still alive as well

---

[1] In addition, there may be no reason at all to wait beyond full retirement age to claim benefits, because spousal benefits do not continue to increase for waiting beyond that point. That is, if a person's benefit as a spouse at full retirement age would be greater than their own retirement benefit at age 70, there's no reason not to go ahead and file at full retirement age.

(because once Allan dies, Liz will switch to her widow's benefit).

Chapter 10 Simple Summary

- For married couples, *both* spouses' respective life expectancies should be considered in *each* spouse's claiming decision.

- It is usually advantageous to have the spouse with the higher primary insurance amount delay claiming his/her retirement benefit as long as possible, because doing so increases the amount the couple will receive as long as *either* spouse is alive.

- For the spouse with the lower primary insurance amount, there's less to be gained as a result of waiting to claim benefits, because doing so only increases the amount the couple will receive while they're *both* alive. (And in some cases there's nothing to be gained from waiting *beyond* full retirement age, because spousal benefits do not continue to increase as a result of waiting past FRA.)

The Restricted Application Strategy for Married Couples

In some cases, there is a strategy available to married couples that (depending on circumstances) might allow them to maximize their Social Security benefits even further.[1]

As we've discussed previously, after reaching full retirement age, if you're eligible for both spousal benefits and your own retirement benefit, you can file a "restricted application" for *just* spousal benefits. This is in contrast to filing for one benefit or the other prior to full retirement age, in which case you would automatically be "deemed" to

---

[1] In addition to the restricted application strategy that we will discuss in this chapter, there is also a "file and suspend" strategy. However, as a result of the Bipartisan Budget Act of 2015, the file and suspend strategy is unavailable unless you already made use of it prior to 4/30/2016. See Appendix B for more information.

have filed for both types of benefits. (As we'll discuss in the next section though, not everybody is eligible to use this restricted application strategy.)

EXAMPLE: Steve and Beth were both born in 1953 and have reached their full retirement age of 66. Beth's earnings history is slightly higher than Steve's. As a result, they chose to have Beth delay her retirement benefit until age 70. However, to help with their near-term cash flow, they chose to have Steve take his benefits at age 62.

Because Beth has reached her full retirement age, she can file a "restricted application" for just her spousal benefit. Later, when Beth reaches age 70, she will file for her own retirement benefit.

Result: Beth receives spousal benefits for four years (from age 66 to 70) at essentially no cost to her, since her own retirement benefit is growing the entire time because she has not yet filed for it. Depending on the size of Steve's primary insurance amount, these four years of spousal benefits could be a large five-figure sum—which Beth and Steve would miss out on entirely if they were less familiar with the Social Security rules.

An important point for people widowed before age 70 is that the deemed filing rules do not apply to widow(er) benefits at all. This opens up two additional restricted application strategies for a person in such circumstances. See Appendix C for more information.

Are You Eligible for a Restricted Application?

As we discussed briefly in Chapter 3, the deemed filing rules are different for anybody who was born after January 1, 1954. For anybody affected by the new rules, deemed filing continues to apply even beyond full retirement age.

As a result, nobody who was born after January 1, 1954 will be able to file a restricted application for spousal benefits. That is, if they file for a spousal benefit at any point, they'll automatically be deemed to have filed for their own retirement benefit as well (assuming they're eligible for one), thereby preventing it from continuing to grow as if they had not yet claimed it.

Chapter 11 Simple Summary

- Via a restricted application, it's often possible for one spouse to receive spousal benefits for the years between full retirement age and age 70, while allowing his/her own retirement benefit to continue growing until age 70.

CHAPTER TWELVE

Accounting for Age Differences Between Spouses

In most cases, the older your spouse is relative to you, the less advantageous it is for you to delay benefits. This is true for two reasons:

1. The older your spouse is when you are age 62 (and first having to decide whether to claim benefits or not), the shorter your joint life expectancy, and
2. If your planned Social Security strategy involves your spouse receiving spousal benefits on your work record, you waiting to claim benefits could cause your spouse to miss out on some years of spousal benefits. (And, in most cases, the older they are relative to you, the more years they miss.)

Both of these concepts are best explained via examples.

EXAMPLE: Carrie and her husband Jim are both age 62. Carrie has a much higher earnings history than Jim. As we've discussed already, it's likely advantageous for Carrie to wait to claim retirement benefits, because waiting increases the amount the couple receives per month as long as either spouse is still alive.

If Jim were 10 years younger than Carrie rather than her same age (i.e., 52 rather than 62), it would be *especially* advantageous for Carrie to delay taking benefits, because the expected length of time for which at least one spouse would still be alive would be quite long.

In contrast, if Jim were 10 years *older* than Carrie (i.e., 72 rather than 62), it would be relatively *less* advantageous for Carrie to delay taking benefits, because the expected length of time for which at least one spouse would still be alive would be relatively shorter.

Jim's decision as the lower-earning spouse is affected by age differences in a very similar manner. That is, the older Carrie is relative to him, the less advantageous it is for him to delay benefits. For example, when Jim is age 62 (and trying to decide whether to claim or wait), the older Carrie is, the shorter the expected length of time for which both spouses will still be alive—and, therefore, the less advantageous it is for him to delay filing.

The other reason that the age difference between two spouses can be so important is that it sometimes causes situations in which one spouse waiting to claim benefits results in the other spouse losing out on spousal benefits in the meantime.

EXAMPLE: Max and Sue are married. They each have a full retirement age of 66. Sue's work history is insufficient to qualify for a retirement benefit of her own.

If Sue is 4 (or more) years younger than Max, Max waiting until age 70 to file for his retirement benefit does not cause Sue to miss any years of full spousal benefits. That is, when she reaches her full retirement age, Max will already be age 70 and collecting benefits, so she can file right away for a full spousal benefit.

If Sue and Max are the same age, Max waiting until age 70 to file for his retirement benefit means that Sue misses out on four years of full spousal benefits (from her full retirement age until age 70) because she has to wait until he is collecting his benefit in order for her to be eligible for spousal benefits.[1]

If Sue is 4 years older than Max, Max waiting until age 70 to file for his retirement benefit causes

---

[1] If Max reached his full retirement age prior to 4/30/2016, there could be an exception, as he could have used the "file and suspend" strategy described in Appendix B.

Sue to miss out on 8 years of full spousal benefits (from her full retirement age until her age 74).

Chapter 12 Simple Summary

- The older your spouse is relative to you, the less desirable it usually is for you to wait to claim benefits.

CHAPTER THIRTEEN

Accounting for Investment Returns

In our discussion up to this point, we've only been looking at the benefits themselves. We have ignored the fact that, in the real world, delaying Social Security usually means spending down your portfolio at a faster rate, which means you are giving up some investment returns as well.

That is, up to this point, we have assumed that when people take benefits early, they're spending those benefits—and therefore spending less from their portfolio per year—and that the additional money left in their portfolio earns a return that matches but does not outpace inflation. (Alternatively, we have been assuming that a person who claims benefits early *invests* the money that they receive, and that the return earned matches but does not outpace inflation.)

And as we've discussed previously, for an unmarried retiree with a full retirement age of 66 and

6 months who is trying to choose between claiming benefits at age 62, or holding off all the way until 70, the breakeven point (assuming a 0% inflation-adjusted return) comes at age 80.5. That is, if the retiree dies before age 80.5, he/she will have been better off taking benefits early at 62. If the retiree lives past age 80.5, he/she will have been better off taking benefits at age 70.

So how does the analysis change when we assume an inflation-adjusted return greater than 0%? The following table shows how the breakeven point changes when we assume a higher rate of return.

Claiming at 62 vs. Claiming at 70 (assuming FRA of 66 and 6 months)	
Inflation-Adjusted Return	Breakeven Age (rounded to nearest year)
0%	80
1%	82
2%	83
3%	85
4%	87
5%	90

As you can see, the higher the after-inflation return that you give up by spending down your portfolio to delay Social Security, the more advantageous it becomes to take benefits early. That's because the "claim at 62" strategy's head start is larger when you account for the investment return that is given up by waiting from 62 to 70. And, naturally, the larger the head start, the longer it takes for the "claim at 70" strategy to close the gap.

So what rate of return are you likely giving up when you spend down assets to delay Social Security? We'll discuss the details further in Chapter 14, but it usually makes most sense to use fixed-income holdings (i.e., bonds, CDs, etc.), to satisfy the additional portfolio-funded spending that's necessary in the pre-Social-Security retirement years. Therefore, the return being given up is usually the (low) return that you would have otherwise earned from those fixed-income holdings. Right now, the yield on the most comparable investment to Social Security (i.e., long-term Treasury Inflation-Protected Securities) is around 1%. So, the 1% row in the table is the one most likely to be applicable in today's environment.

As mentioned earlier, according to the Social Security Administration, the total life expectancy at age 62 is 82 for a male and 84.8 for a female. Point being: Even after accounting for forgone investment returns, most people live past the applicable breakeven point. This is *one* reason (not the only reason) why most people will benefit by delaying benefits.

There is no way to present the breakeven points for married people in a simple table, because they vary significantly depending on both the age difference between the spouses and on the difference between the spouses' PIAs. As with unmarried people though, the key point is that the higher the rate of return you give up when spending down your portfolio, the later the breakeven point.[1]

Why Spend Down Fixed-Income?

Spending down your bond holdings in order to delay filing can be thought of as swapping one fixed-income asset for another. But the fixed-income asset that you're getting a) usually provides a better return than the asset that you're giving up and b) helps reduce longevity risk. In a majority of cases, that's an advantageous exchange.[2]

If you were to spend down stock holdings in order to "buy more" Social Security, you would be exchanging an asset with high risk and high expected return for one with low risk and modest

---

[1] One difference, however, is that for a married couple, for it to make sense for the high-PIA spouse to delay, only *one* spouse needs to make it to the point at which the high-PIA spouse would have been the age in question. Conversely, for it to make sense for the low-PIA spouse to delay, *both* spouses would need to survive until the applicable breakeven point.

[2] If you're interested in research relating to spending down bonds to delay Social Security, you may want to read either or both of two papers: "Optimizing Retirement Income by Integrating Retirement Plans, IRAs, and Home Equity" by Wade Pfau, Joe Tomlinson, and Steve Vernon or "Anuitized Income and Optimal Equity Allocation" by David Blanchett and Michael Finke.

expected return. That *might* be advantageous for you, especially if you need the longevity risk protection (i.e., you are concerned about outliving your money). But it's not as clear of a "win" as spending down bonds and other fixed-income holdings to delay Social Security.

Chapter 13 Simple Summary

- The higher the inflation-adjusted rate of return you can earn on your money, the more advantageous it becomes to claim benefits early, in order to allow more of your portfolio to remain invested.

- When spending down a portfolio to delay claiming Social Security, it usually makes most sense to spend down fixed-income holdings to the extent possible and practical. In doing so, you're essentially swapping one fixed-income asset for another such asset—one that usually provides a better return *and* helps reduce longevity risk.

- Because it is bond holdings that are typically spent down in order to delay Social Security, the return that is given up is usually fairly modest.

PART FOUR

Other Related Retirement-Planning Topics

CHAPTER FOURTEEN

Social Security and Asset Allocation

Most advice about constructing and managing a retirement portfolio assumes that you'll be spending the same amount of money from your portfolio each year (after accounting for inflation). This assumption is decidedly unrealistic for anybody who doesn't intend to claim Social Security immediately upon retiring.

So how should you make use of the traditional advice if your retirement date does not coincide with the date on which you will begin receiving Social Security? One reasonable answer: Consider mentally separating your portfolio into two portfolios. One is constructed using the typical advice (e.g., a diversified portfolio of low-cost index funds), and it is used to satisfy a steady level of spending throughout your retirement. The other, which is invested in something safe (e.g., a CD ladder or short-term bond fund) is used to satisfy the additional portfolio-funded spending that is necessary prior to your Social Security benefit(s) kicking in.

As you may have noticed, this strategy coincides nicely with the observation from Chapter 13 that it is usually advantageous to spend primarily from fixed-income holdings in order to fund delaying Social Security.

EXAMPLE: Roger is planning to retire at age 62. But because he has a family history of longevity, he has decided to wait until age 70 to claim his Social Security retirement benefit. Roger expects his retirement spending needs to total approximately $50,000 per year. When Roger collects Social Security at age 70, his annual benefit will be $22,000. Roger has no sources of income other than his portfolio and his Social Security.

Rather than spending an equal amount from his portfolio each year, Roger will be spending $50,000 per year for eight years (from age 62 to 70). Then, from age 70 onward, he'll only be spending $28,000 per year ($50,000 minus his $22,000 annual benefit).

Roger might find it beneficial to mentally separate his assets into two distinct portfolios. One portfolio will be used to satisfy $22,000 of expenses per year for eight years (until his Social Security kicks in). The other portfolio will need to satisfy $28,000 of expenses every year, starting immediately upon retirement, for the remainder of Roger's life.

Because Roger's first portfolio will be entirely depleted within eight years, it should probably be invested in something very safe. Perhaps a low-risk bond fund would be a good choice, or maybe a CD ladder consisting of eight roughly equally-sized CDs (one maturing each year for eight years).

Roger's second portfolio will consist of the remainder of his financial assets. Because this portfolio is intended to satisfy an approximately steady level of spending ($28,000 per year), the conventional advice *would* apply. That is, Roger would probably benefit from constructing a diversified, low-cost portfolio (of low-cost index funds or ETFs, for example) using an asset allocation that's suitable for his risk tolerance. Alternatively, if he is particularly risk-averse, Roger might find it beneficial to allocate a portion of this money to a lifetime inflation-adjusted annuity.

By mentally dividing his portfolio like this, Roger can easily see how much to put into very safe investments to satisfy his near-term spending needs for the years prior to collecting Social Security (in this case, approximately $176,000, or $22,000 for each of eight years) and how much to invest using a more long-term-oriented allocation.

For married couples, there is more complexity involved given that the two spouses will usually retire at different points in time and they will often claim Social Security at different points in time as well. But the general concept is the same: Make sure that you have enough safe assets to get you through to the point at which you'll start collecting Social Security. The remainder of the portfolio, which will be spent over a more extended period of time, can be invested more aggressively (though many retirees will still prefer to invest this part of the portfolio relatively conservatively).

Chapter 14 Simple Summary

- When deciding the asset allocation for your retirement portfolio, it can be helpful to think of it as two separate portfolios: one (invested very conservatively) that you will spend down in the years of retirement prior to collecting Social Security and one (invested more aggressively) that you will use for the remainder of your spending needs throughout your entire retirement.

CHAPTER FIFTEEN

Checking Your Earnings Record

The Social Security Administration used to send a statement each year that showed your earnings record by year, as well as an estimate of what your Social Security retirement benefit would be if you claimed it at age 62, at full retirement age, or at age 70.

Those mailed statements have largely been replaced, however, by an online statement, available at ssa.gov/myaccount (after you jump through some hoops to verify your identity, that is). Today, statements are only mailed to people age 60 and over who are not yet receiving benefits and who have not created an online Social Security account.

Checking Your Earnings Record

In addition to being helpful for the purpose of getting an estimate of your Social Security retirement benefits, creating an account on the Social Security website is helpful because it allows you to check your earnings record. Mistakes happen, and it's best to get them fixed as quickly as possible.

However, according to the SSA, if your record is missing earnings from this year or last year, it's usually not a problem. Most likely, it simply means that the earnings haven't been recorded just yet. They should appear on a later statement.

Correcting Mistakes in Your Earnings Record

If you find that your earnings record is missing earnings (other than those from this year or last year), you'll want to find something that documents the correct amount of earnings, such as:

- Your Form 1040 from the year in question,
- Applicable Forms W-2,
- Applicable pay stubs, or
- If you were self-employed, Schedule C or Schedule SE from that year.

Once you've found something documenting your earnings, you'll want to call the SSA to get things straightened out as soon as possible.

Where to Find Earnings Documentation

If you no longer have anything documenting your earnings for the year in question, you could call your employer from that year to request your W-2 or, failing that, some other sort of payroll record.

Alternatively, you can order a transcript of that year's tax return from the IRS. A tax return transcript includes most information that was filed on your return for the year, including any accompanying schedules or forms. You can request a transcript in any of three ways:

1. Calling the IRS at 800-908-9946,
2. Ordering it online[1], or
3. Sending in Form 4506-T.

If you worked as an employee, the figure that should show up for a given year's earnings record on the Social Security website is the number from box 3 ("Social Security wages") from your Form W-2 for the year. If you had multiple jobs, it should be the total of all your box 3's (limited to the maximum earnings subject to Social Security tax for the year). The reason they don't use box 1 is that the calculation for box 1 includes reductions for things like pre-tax 401(k) contributions, which reduce income taxes but not Social Security taxes.

---

[1] You can do this at:
irs.gov/individuals/get-transcript

If you were self-employed, the figure that should appear on your Social Security earnings record is line 4 ("net earnings from self-employment") from Schedule SE. Note that this amount is not the same as the profit from your business. Rather, it's 92.35% of the profit from your business, to account for the deduction you get for one-half of your self-employment tax.

Chapter 15 Simple Summary

- By creating an account on the Social Security website (at ssa.gov/myaccount), you can get an estimate of your retirement benefits and you can check your earnings record for errors.

- In the event that you do find an error in your earnings record, you'll want to send the SSA proof of your actual earnings from that year. If you don't have any such proof, and cannot get any from your employer, you can contact the IRS to get a transcript of the applicable tax return.

CHAPTER SIXTEEN

How Is Social Security Taxed?

Each year, the portion of your Social Security income that's subject to federal income tax depends on your "combined income." Your combined income is equal to:

- Your adjusted gross income (currently line 7 on the second page of your Form 1040), not including any Social Security benefits, plus
- Any tax-exempt interest you earned, plus
- 50% of your Social Security benefits.

If your combined income is below $25,000 ($32,000 if married filing jointly), none of your Social Security benefits will be taxed.

For every dollar of combined income above that level, $0.50 of benefits will become taxable until 50% of your benefits are taxed or until you reach

$34,000 of combined income ($44,000 if married filing jointly).

For every dollar of combined income above $34,000 ($44,000 if married filing jointly), $0.85 of Social Security benefits will become taxable—all the way up to the point at which 85% of your Social Security benefits are taxable.[1]

Important note: To say that 85% of your Social Security benefits are taxable does not mean that 85% of your benefits will disappear to taxes. Rather, it means that 85% of your benefits will be included as taxable income when determining your total income tax for the year.

How Does This Affect Tax and Retirement Planning?

The big takeaway of the above calculations is that, once you start collecting Social Security, your marginal tax rate on ordinary income (i.e., the tax rate you would pay on each additional dollar of income) often increases dramatically. That's because, if your "combined income" is in the applicable range, each additional dollar of income is not only taxed at your regular tax rate, it also causes an additional $0.50 or $0.85 of Social Security benefits to be taxable.

---

[1] These are the general rules. As with so many aspects of the tax code, there are exceptions. For more information, see IRS Publication 915, at: irs.gov/publications/p915

This change in your marginal tax rate often creates significant tax planning opportunities.

For example, if you haven't yet begun to collect Social Security and you realize that your marginal tax rate will increase once you do, you may benefit from funding most of your current spending via withdrawals from tax-deferred accounts (as opposed to taxable accounts or Roth accounts), thereby allowing the withdrawals to be taxed at your current, relatively-lower marginal tax rate, and thereby preserving your Roth accounts for funding spending needs in the future when your marginal tax rate will be higher.

Or you might even want to take it one step further by converting a portion of your traditional IRA(s) to a Roth IRA in the years of retirement prior to collecting Social Security.

Or, if you are already collecting Social Security, once your combined income nears the range where Social Security benefits will start to become taxable, you may want to fund the rest of your spending (to the extent possible) with assets *not* from tax-deferred accounts (so as to stay below the range where your benefits would become taxable).

Alternatively, if your combined income is already near the *high* end of the range in question (such that most or all of your benefits are 85% taxable), it may make sense to withdraw *more* from your tax-deferred accounts (perhaps just enough to put you up to the top of your current tax bracket) so that you can withdraw less next year, thereby allowing you to stay in the range where some of your benefits will not be taxable.

Chapter 16 Simple Summary

• Depending on how high your "combined income" is in a given year, your Social Security benefits could be nontaxable or partially taxable (with up to 85% being included in your taxable income for the year).

• If it looks like your marginal tax rate is going to increase sharply once you start collecting Social Security, it may make sense—in the years prior to collecting Social Security—to fund much of your spending from tax-deferred accounts (and potentially execute Roth IRA conversions) to take advantage of the fact that your marginal tax rate is lower than it will be in the future.

• Once you start collecting Social Security, you may be able to reduce your overall tax bill by carefully planning *which* accounts you spend from each year (tax-deferred as opposed to Roth as opposed to taxable) so as to minimize the portion of your Social Security benefits that will be taxable.

CHAPTER SEVENTEEN

Do-Over Options

At some point, you may wish that you could change your mind with regard to when you claimed Social Security benefits. Fortunately, there are a few options that may help in such cases.

Withdrawing Your Application

If you have been receiving benefits for less than 12 months and you change your mind about having filed, you can withdraw your application by filing Form SSA-521 and paying back all benefits you have received to date as well as any other benefits paid out on your work record (e.g., spousal benefits paid to your spouse). If your withdrawal request is approved, it will be as if you had never filed at all. Of note: You can only withdraw an application once in your lifetime.

EXAMPLE: Beth files for benefits on her 64th birthday. Seven months later, she changes her mind and decides she'd rather wait until age 70. By filing Form SSA-521 and paying back all the benefits she's received so far, she can essentially undo her application, thereby allowing her Social Security benefit to grow until age 70.

It's worth noting, however, that the withdrawal of application process is not as easy as that one-page form makes it look, due to the fact that many SSA employees are not particularly familiar with the process. In addition, there can be tax ramifications resulting from the repayment of benefits that you received in a prior year.[1]

Suspending Retirement Benefits

If you've been receiving benefits for 12 months or more, it's not possible to pay back your benefits and start over. Once you reach full retirement age, however, you can ask to have your benefits "suspended," thereby allowing your retirement benefit to grow as if you hadn't yet filed for it.

EXAMPLE: Greg's full retirement age is 67, and his primary insurance amount is $1,600. He begins claiming benefits at age 62, meaning that he

---

[1] See IRS Publication 915 for more information: irs.gov/publications/p915

receives $1,120 per month (that is, 70% of his PIA due to claiming five years early).

Three years later, he changes his mind and wishes he had waited. Once he reaches his full retirement age of 67, he can have his benefits suspended. If he waits until age 70 to start them again, he'll earn 3 years' worth of "delayed retirement credits," increasing his benefit by 8% for each year he waits, or 24% in total. Starting at age 70, Greg will receive $1,388 per month (calculated as his $1,600 PIA, times 70%, times 124%).

Social Security Earnings Test

If you claim benefits early and change your mind after missing the 12-month window but before reaching your full retirement age, there's still one thing you can do that will help you offset the effect of claiming early: work.

As we discussed in Chapter 8, in years prior to full retirement age during which you work while claiming benefits, the Social Security earnings test will reduce your annual benefit by $1 for every $2 by which your annual earnings exceed a certain amount ($17,640 in 2019).

Then, after you reach full retirement age, your benefit will be recalculated to account for the benefits you didn't receive earlier. For example, if the earnings test resulted in a reduced or eliminated benefit for ten months, your benefit after full retirement age will be calculated as if you'd claimed ten months later than you actually did.[1]

Backdating a Claim for Benefits

Alternatively, if you decide at some point that you wish you had claimed benefits *earlier* (whether retirement benefits, spousal benefits, widow(er) benefits or child benefits), you can request in your application that you receive benefits for up to six months prior to the month in which you actually file your application. Note, however, that you cannot receive benefits in this way for:

- A month in which you were not eligible for benefits, or
- A month prior to the month in which you reach your full retirement age. (This exception does not apply for child benefits.)[2]

---

[1] When recalculating your benefits at FRA, the SSA accounts for any month in which you didn't receive a full benefit. So if the earnings test eliminated your benefit for nine months, and cut it in half for a tenth month, your benefit at FRA would be recalculated as if you had missed ten months of benefits.

[2] In certain cases in which disability is involved, spousal benefits and widow(er) benefits may be retroactively obtained for up to *twelve* months. See 404.621 of the Code of Federal Regulations for more information: ssa.gov/OP_Home/cfr20/404/404-0621.htm

For example, if you first file for retirement benefits in October of a given year and you decide that you should have filed for benefits earlier, you can effectively backdate your application to April (six months prior to October). If, however, you reached your full retirement age in July of that year, July would be the earliest month to which you could backdate your application.

Chapter 17 Simple Summary

- If you have been receiving benefits for less than 12 months, it's possible to "undo" your application by filing a withdrawal of application form and paying back the benefits you've received to date.

- If you claimed benefits early and changed your mind (and you're past the 12-month window), you can increase your future monthly benefit by working prior to full retirement age (thereby subjecting your benefits to the earnings test), or by having payments suspended between full retirement age and age 70.

- When you first file for retirement, spousal, or widow(er) benefits, you can choose to backdate your application by up to six months (but no earlier than the month in which you reached full retirement age).

Six Social Security Rules of Thumb

Unfortunately, the Social Security rules can be bewilderingly complex. And to determine the very best claiming strategy for your family, you would have to understand how those rules interact with a whole list of variables, the most important of which—the age at which you (and your spouse if you're married) will die—is entirely unknowable.

Fortunately, there are six rules of thumb that can get you most of the way there.

RULE #1: The longer you expect to live (or the more worried you are about running out of money if you do live to have a long retirement), the better it is to hold off on taking benefits.

RULE #2: For an unmarried person trying to decide between claiming as early as possible at age 62 or as late as possible at age 70, the breakeven point is approximately age 80.5. That is, if the person lives beyond that point, he/she will have received more total benefits by waiting until 70 rather than claiming early. (And, for reference, the average total life expectancy for a 62-year-old is age 83.4.)

RULE #3 In a married couple, having the person with the higher primary insurance amount delay benefits increases the amount the couple will receive per month as long as *either* spouse is alive. (And, generally speaking, this makes it advantageous for the higher earner to delay benefits.)

RULE #4: In a married couple, having the spouse with the lower primary insurance amount delay benefits only increases the amount the couple will receive per month while *both* spouses are still alive. Naturally, this makes it relatively less advantageous for this person to hold off on taking benefits. (That said, it could still be a good idea if both spouses expect to live a long time or if the couple is particularly afraid of running out of money during retirement.)

RULE #5: There is often a way for one spouse to receive a few years of "free" benefits: by filing a restricted application for just spousal benefits at full retirement age, while allowing his/her own retirement benefit to continue growing until age 70.

RULE #6: The higher the after-inflation rate of return you can earn on your investments (especially your fixed-income investments), the better it becomes to take Social Security early, so you do not have to spend down your portfolio as quickly. As a result, if inflation-adjusted interest rates are very high (which, as I write this, they are not), you may be better off taking the money early.

Please remember, however, that these are just general guidelines. There are many factors involved in Social Security-related decisions, and depending on your circumstances, it may be best to break one or more of these rules. When in doubt, seek the assistance of a knowledgeable financial planner.

Appendix A

Widow(er) Benefits: Math Details

When a widow(er) claims widow(er) benefits prior to full retirement age, the amount he/she receives is reduced. If the deceased spouse had not claimed his/her retirement benefit prior to full retirement age, the surviving spouse's benefit will be reduced by 28.5% if he/she claims widow(er) benefits as early as possible (at age 60). And the amount he/she receives will increase from there on a pro-rata basis for each month closer he/she is to full retirement age when he/she claims widow(er) benefits.

If, however, the surviving spouse claims widow(er) benefits prior to full retirement age, and the deceased spouse *had* claimed his/her retirement benefit prior to full retirement age, the calculation is different. The starting point for the calculation is now the deceased spouse's PIA rather than the amount that the deceased spouse was receiving at death. From there, the same reduction (e.g., 28.5% if claimed at age 60) will apply. However, the resulting benefit is then limited to the greater of:

- 82.5% of the deceased spouse's PIA, or

- The amount the deceased spouse was receiving at the time of his/her death.

In other words, from the point of view of a worker, just as delaying claiming benefits *increases* what your widow(er) can collect, claiming early *reduces* what your widow(er) can collect, but not below 82.5% of your PIA. However, if your widow(er) then claims widow(er) benefits before full retirement age, the resulting amount can be below 82.5% of your PIA.

File and Suspend Strategies

What follows is a description of the "file and suspend" strategies that were popular for several years. As we'll discuss momentarily, however, the Bipartisan Budget Act of 2015 eliminated these strategies for anybody who had not already suspended their benefits as of 4/29/2016 or earlier.

"File and Suspend" to Allow a Spouse to Receive Spousal Benefits

If you have reached full retirement age, you can apply for your own retirement benefit, then ask to have payments suspended. Under the old voluntary suspension rules, this satisfied the requirement that you must have claimed your own benefit in order for your spouse to receive a spouse's benefit. And because you were not actually *receiving* your own retirement benefit, your benefit would continue to grow until age 70.

EXAMPLE: Katie and Joe are married. They both reached their full retirement age of 66 in early 2016. Joe has earned more than Katie over the course of their careers—so much more, in fact, that Katie's spousal benefit is almost twice the size of her own retirement benefit.

Katie and Joe chose to have the higher earner (Joe) wait until 70 and the lower earner (Katie) claim as early as possible at age 62. So far, this is the same as the "restricted application" strategy outlined in Chapter 11. At full retirement age, however, the strategies diverge.

At Joe's full retirement age, instead of filing a restricted application for just spousal benefits, he filed for his *own* benefit and asked to have payments immediately suspended. This allowed Katie to switch to her (larger) spousal benefit, and it allows Joe's own retirement benefit (and Katie's survivor benefit, if she should outlive him) to continue growing until Joe reaches age 70.

Combining Restricted Application with File and Suspend

If both spouses wanted to delay their own retirement benefit until age 70, under the old voluntary suspension rules it was often possible to combine the restricted application strategy and the file and suspend strategy in order to get 3-4 years of drawback-free spousal benefits for one spouse.

EXAMPLE: Christopher and Patricia are married, and they both reached their full retirement age of 66 in early 2016. They have similar earnings histories, and they both want to delay their retirement benefits until age 70.

Upon reaching full retirement age, Patricia filed for benefits and asked to have payments immediately suspended. Christopher (who had also reached full retirement age) then filed a restricted application for spousal benefits only. At age 70 Christopher will switch to his own retirement benefit, and Patricia will end the suspension of her benefit payments.

Result: Christopher will be able to receive spousal benefits for four years (from age 66 to 70), while they both allow their own retirement benefits to grow until age 70.

Retroactively Unsuspending Benefits

Under the old voluntary suspension rules, filing and suspending could also be useful as a way to give yourself another "change your mind" option down the road. Specifically, if you had filed for retirement benefits and asked for those benefits to be suspended, you could later *un*suspend and ask to have all or some of the benefits from the date of suspension onward paid as a lump sum. Your ongoing monthly benefit would then be reduced as if you had originally started receiving benefits on that earlier date.

In other words, this was a way to retroactively change your mind—all the way back to full retirement age if you filed and suspended right away at full retirement age.

Because of this ability, an unmarried person who planned to wait until age 70 to take retirement benefits could file and suspend at full retirement age, just to preserve the opportunity to change his/her mind later. (Ditto for a married person who did not plan to take retirement or spousal benefits prior to age 70.)

Are You Eligible for File and Suspend Strategies?

As a result of the Bipartisan Budget Act of 2015, most people are no longer eligible for the file and suspend strategies described above. Specifically, unless your request to suspend benefits occurred prior to 4/30/2016, then the rules are different in three ways:

1. You will not be able to receive a benefit based on anybody else's work record while your benefits are suspended,
2. Nobody else (except an ex-spouse) will be able to receive a benefit based on your work record while your benefits are suspended, and
3. There will no longer be the option to retroactively unsuspend as a sort of "change your mind" strategy.

For anybody affected, these second and third changes essentially eliminated the popular "file and suspend" strategies.

Appendix C

Restricted Applications with Widow(er) Benefits

Prior to reaching full retirement age, if you are eligible for your own retirement benefit and a spousal benefit, and you file for either of the two, you are automatically "deemed" to have filed for the other benefit as well. You have no choice in the matter.

After reaching full retirement age, however, deemed filing no longer applies. (At least, that's the case for people not affected by the Bipartisan Budget Act of 2015's new rules.) And that's why the typical restricted application strategy starts at full retirement age rather than at age 62. For example, after reaching full retirement age, one spouse can file a restricted application for spousal benefits only while allowing his/her own retirement benefit to continue growing until age 70.

Deemed Filing Doesn't Apply to Widow(er) Benefits

The deemed filing rule does not, however, apply to widow(er) benefits. (And, just to be clear, this has not been changed as a result of the Bipartisan

Budget Act of 2015.) As a result, there are two possible Social Security claiming strategies that often make sense for somebody whose spouse has passed away:

1. At age 60, you could claim a widow(er) benefit while allowing your own retirement benefit to grow until 70, or
2. You could claim your own retirement benefit at 62 while allowing your widow(er) benefit to grow until full retirement age.

The first thing you'll want to do is calculate your maximum widow(er) benefit (i.e., your widow(er) benefit if you wait until full retirement age to claim it) and your maximum retirement benefit (i.e., your retirement benefit if you wait until age 70 to claim it). Whichever of those two amounts is smaller is typically the benefit that you should claim as early as possible, while you then allow the other benefit to grow until it maxes out (either at FRA or at age 70, depending upon which benefit it is).

Acknowledgements

As always, my thanks go to my editing team: Michelle, Pat, Debbi, and Kalinda. Thank you once again.

In addition, my sincere gratitude goes to Albert Kinderman and Jim Blankenship, CFP, EA for contributing their time as technical editors, as well as to the anonymous sscritic of the Bogleheads investment forum and Jewell Colbert of the Social Security Administration for taking the time to answer my questions.

Also by Mike Piper

Accounting Made Simple: Accounting Explained in 100 Pages or Less

Cost Accounting Made Simple: Cost Accounting Explained in 100 Pages or Less

Can I Retire? How to Manage Your Retirement Savings, Explained in 100 Pages or Less

Independent Contractor, Sole Proprietor, and LLC Taxes Explained in 100 Pages or Less

Investing Made Simple: Investing in Index Funds Explained in 100 Pages or Less

LLC vs. S-Corp vs. C-Corp Explained in 100 Pages or Less

Microeconomics Made Simple: Basic Microeconomic Principles Explained in 100 Pages or Less

Taxes Made Simple: Income Taxes Explained in 100 Pages or Less

About the Author

Mike is the author of several books as well as the popular blog ObliviousInvestor.com. He is a Missouri licensed CPA. Mike's writing has been featured in many places, including *The Wall Street Journal*, *Money*, *Forbes*, and *MarketWatch*.

INDEX

CPSIA information can be obtained
at www.ICGtesting.com
Printed in the USA
LVHW111015051119
636371LV00007B/364/P